Where Pelicans Fly

A celebration of the extraordinary everyday

photography and text by

Paul Sinrud Johnson

ISBN-13: 978-1479309580

in memory of
Corinne Frances Johnson Link
beloved sister

Prologue

As the seasons change, so also does the landscape that surrounds us, including forests, fields, water, and the creatures within. No two months or weeks are alike. My home in central Missouri fulfills this promise of the earth and nature. Some may see it as ordinary and others perhaps not at all. But my years have brought me closer to it now – as I become increasingly aware of how extraordinary it all is. Photographing the *extraordinary everyday*, as I call it, has become the lodestar and touchstone to all of nature around me.

American white pelicans migrate through my area during late winter and spring, and again in autumn. Their presence forms the bookends of my photographic year. The 9-foot wing span of these quiet, gentle, and social creatures are the second-longest among all North American birds (after the California Condor). I find the pelicans irresistably photogenic and impossible to ignore while they are here. But after they depart, the landscape, sunsets, and other wildlife remain. These subjects provide the images and inspiration for the following pages.

The photos are from that part of Boone County lying along or near the Missouri River. This includes the nearby rolling uplands that form a mosaic of oak forests and fields, as well as the alluvial wetlands adjacent to the river. Most of the wildlife images are from Eagle Bluffs Conservation Area, a 4,400-acre state-owned wetland managed by the Missouri Department of Conservation. Although the area is managed for multiple uses, migratory waterfowl protection and regulated hunting are of key importance. The area includes a series of shallow ponds and levees with control structures for managing water levels. The need for such designed wildlife areas is a consequence of the disappearance of natural wetlands along the Missouri River and elsewhere in the Midwest. Without this and other state and federal lands like it, many of the wildlife species represented in these pages might now occur only in greatly reduced numbers or perhaps not at all. Many of the wildlife ponds at Eagle Bluffs are bordered by cropland managed in part for wildlife food. This, together with other wetland vegetation including bottomland hardwood forests, cattail marshes, and grasslands, form the matrix of food, cover and water essential to the migrating birds and other wildlife that live there.

We are a part of that *something* we call nature. If we choose, we can become intimate with it in our backyards and nearby parks, as well as in distant wildernesses. But wherever we find it, it has already found us. Our connections to nature are embedded in our evolutionary history and thus dwell within the fabric of our being. Among all the creatures on earth, humans are the only species (as far as we know) that possess an awareness of the 'other', i.e. that something beyond ourselves we have chosen to call nature. From this gift of awareness we can grow individually and societally toward a greater appreciation and understanding of nature's significance to our well being.

Consciously or not, we may exclude ourselves from that something we call *nature*. But by so doing, the *something* becomes 'not us'. In perceiving nature this way, we distance ourselves from it. This distancing arises from the habit of positioning ourselves as subject (*I*) viewing the rest of the world as object (*it*). From our earliest years, we have been taught to think in this way – submerged in the *It*-world. This mode of thought, or consciousness, forms the cornerstone of our objective analysis of virtually everything we encounter. It is the foundation of the scientific method and how we experience and use the phenomenal world through analysis and classification.

Above:: Panaromic view of the Missouri River looking eastward toward Eagle Bluffs Conservation Area in Boone County..

But when we do this, explains philosopher Martin Buber, we stand (exist) in the "realm of *I-It*." From that position, the *I-It* monopolizes our consciousness. However, Buber explains, there is another realm of existence (or mode of consciousness): the *I-Thou*. Although more difficult to explain than the *I-It*, the *I-Thou* can be described as:

> Myself (*I*) responding completely and uniquely to something outside myself, i.e. an 'other' (a *Thou*) that has come into my presence. In this context, *Thou* refers neither to God nor anything else theological.

But to fully grasp the meaning of *I-Thou* it must foremost be understood as:

> A *relationship*, and one that is reciprocal and characterized by a unique and genuine dialogue between myself and an 'other' to whom I make myself fully present. In contrast, an *I-It* relation is monological and detached.

Nature is but one category of the 'other' with which genuine dialogue can occur. Such dialogue also can occur between persons, and between persons and art, writing, music and other creations resulting from meetings with a *Thou*. An *I-Thou* dialogue between persons is directly exchanged through language, but between man and nature is received from below the threshold of language. Moreover, the two realms of existence, *I-It* and *I-Thou*, alternate such that we remain in either only temporarily. Buber emphasizes that we are only truly human to the extent that we are capable of genuine dialogue with a *Thou*. Moreover, it is through *I-Thou* dialogue that we can glimpse the *Eternal Thou*, which is the *Thou* that can never become an *It*.* The *I-It* nevertheless is necessary for our functioning in everyday life so that we can attend to the practical necessities required for our livelihood and physical survival.

Discovering the extraordinary everyday requires freeing oneself of *I-It* monologue and entering into *I-Thou* dialogue. In turn, this requires 'seeing' the whole rather than the details of that which we encounter. Recognizing and addressing this wholeness thus stands in opposition to the reductionist *I-It*. Various phrases and analogies have been used to facilitate conceptualizing this. These include expressions such as 'the unity of a thing', 'seeing

---

*Buber tells us that the *Eternal Thou* can be glimpsed in genuine *I-Thou* relationships. Moreover, this *Thou* is met by anyone who adresses God by any name, and even by one who does not believe in God yet addresses the *Thous* of his life (Friedman).

everything equally', 'inseparably fused' and similar. The actualization of such perceptions arises through a deeper relationship with the phenomenal world that only can be obtained through abstraction. An example is provided by the adage: "The whole is greater than the sum of its parts." In this sense, the whole can never be objectified, only imagined – meaning that something more than the sensory or measurable is involved. Expressed another way, things (especially living beings) intuitively lose their holistic essence when reduced to their component parts. In Buber's dialogical context, these components are not addressable. In contrast, I can address (interact with) a tree or an owl in its entirety, i.e. in its greater completeness including its interactions with other elements of nature. The resulting relationship I have with an 'other', according to Buber, comprises a *lived experience*. Stepping into this mode of consciousness requires removing the observing self to allow the possibility of genuine dialogue with the 'other'. But having done so does not imply that we are one with nature – nor that we should aspire to be. On the contrary, it is from the two sides of the *I-Thou* encounter that dialogue is possible.

My own dialogues with nature are perhaps better described as 'silent conversations' – from which I neither anticipate nor receive direct reply. Nevertheless, I sense that a response is virtually always obtained – albeit in a formative way. Because these conversations influence my consciousness, over time they shape who I am; they remain a presence within me. Like engaging in genuine dialogue with another person, it is difficult to understand how it could be otherwise. So whether a response is instantaneous, long-delayed, or seldom received, this mode of consciousness is neither mysterious, mystical, nor inaccessible. It is accessible to all. Nevertheless, the *I-Thou* often lies only dimly lit beneath the *I-It* that so frequently monopolizes our consciousness.

Above: Martin Buber (from a German postage stamp commemorating his life, 1878-1965).

A genuine personal relationship with nature also impels social and moral responsibilities. These are two-fold and entwined: first, to take responsibility for one's own nature education – which is primarily an *I-It* enterprise; and second, to share that knowledge and understanding with others – preferably and whenever possible through agenda-free *I-Thou* dialogue of shared mutuality. How else will it be possible for us to intelligently care for the earth? Certainly not out of a collective ignorance and indifference to nature. And care of the earth, our home, is a corollary of the golden rule with consequences extending to future generations. We have no 'second home'. To this end, my admonition to anyone with an environmental conscience is to become intimate with nature. Although Buber's dialogical model works for me, there is no universal formula. Follow your own path; just be sure to make the connection and have the conversation.

As I watch the river birch in the backyard nodding in the evening breeze, I nod back, but not so much physically as mindfully. In that moment, I'm reminded that the tree and I share a common home, earth, and that we are born of a common evolutionary process. We are separate and unique, yet unified as parts of a singular oneness. Through this silent conversation with the tree, the moment has become a part of my extraordinary everyday.

Sunset over floodwaters, Missouri River floodplain

Pelican flight

As they pass low overhead, I can hear them talking to each other, and am wont to believe they are speaking to me too.

Colony of cliff swallows nest-building on a concrete bridge. Their nests are constructed from wet mud from the river margins below.

Hallow the moment for it will never reoccur.

Out of a darkening afternoon light, the pelicans dropped in to fill my moment with fascination and beauty – and to remind me that we are not the lone inhabitants of this earth. To our own fullfilment, it is a home we share with them and many other creatures.

Late afternoon gathering

Mallard drake

As we become more intimate with nature, our dialogue with it becomes ever more likely to elicit a response. But any response received, though lying below the threshold of language, will be enduring and formative.

As shadows lengthen and the light softens to red, evening descends like a benediction to prepare earth's creatures for tomorrow's journey.

Pelicans at eventide

Bald eagle

Science and economics has told us much about the measurable costs and benefits of both human-caused and natural events that affect nature – and thereby mankind. But they have told us little about how looking into the eye of an eagle or an owl affects us psychologically and spiritually. Those effects are not included in the calculation of the gross domestic product – which alone is considered by many as the bottom line in defining our well being.

The death of the canary in the mine is an alarm to all within. Yet we seem deaf to the alarms set off by the extinctions, near extinctions and loss of habitats of wild species struggling to maintain a toehold on this earth. Is it not time to wake up?

Barred owl

Landscape colors under a changing sky along the Missouri River bottoms.

Every day in every moment that you can, marvel at the clouds and sky and how they change. We are given the gift to observe, ponder and treasure all this if we but choose to do so.

On their way westward, Lewis and Clark passed this point on June 5, 1804. Their expedition was, by all accounts, a journey of discovery. In our own journey, discoveries similarly await us. They are accessible to us any time, any place, through our potentially unlimited and continually expanding human consciousness. Therein lies our capacity to make the everyday extraordinary.

The Missouri River looking northeast from atop a bluff on its west bank in Moniteau County. The north end of Eagle Bluffs Conservation Area in Boone County lies on the far bank; photo June 1, 2012 (208 years after Lewis and Clark passed by on the westward leg of their expedition).

Belted kingfisher

Perhaps someday, before it's too late, we'll recognize the need for everyone to become nature literate. Like other educational endeavors, we don't all have to attain the same level of knowledge of nature – or even hold the same view of it. There is even value in 'knowing what you don't know', i.e. the paradox of becoming, through learning, more acutely aware of the depth of one's ignorance.

Although few of us will find true wilderness in our backyard, many can find wildness there. Nature persists wherever habitats – even tiny microsms – are available to wild things. The side-by-side coexistence of humans and wildlife is the norm throughout most of suburban America. There, backyards, local parks and even empty lots often abound in wild things – as well as in nearby rural communities and farms. Nature is irrepressible and surrounds us. We have only to open our eyes to become aware of nature, then engage it. An absence of true wilderness or expansive areas of near-wilderness therefore is not a valid explanation of, nor excuse for, a societal or personal deficit in nature literacy.

Pied-billed grebe

Great egrets

When we speak the word 'nature' to another, we probably assume a common understanding of it. But should we? Its meaning is enveloped in ambiguity. My various lexicons list more than 20 definitions and connotations in attempting to cover the word's complete sense. Perhaps the following excerpt from Goethe's incomparable essay (ca. 1780) captures the essence and magnitude of the ambiguity: "NATURE! We are surrounded and embraced by her: powerless to separate ourselves from her, and powerless to penetrate beyond her... We live in her midst and know her not. She is incessantly speaking to us, but betrays not her secret. We constantly act upon her, and yet have no power over her.... Each of her works has an essence of its own; each of her phenomena is a special characterization: and yet their diversity is in unity."

A pair of sandhill cranes with a great blue heron (left). Normally gray in color, the rusty brown of these cranes (observed in early June) is reportedly the result of preening with mud-stained bills. By late summer, the stained feathers molt and their plumage returns to gray. The species occurs as an occassional migrant in my area.

Northern shoveler (male)

Though we see nature and landscapes with our eyes, these images are then processed by the mind. What we ultimately internalize is therefore likely to differ among us. Yet we are social creatures, unique among all others in recognizing that our individual and collective well being depends on coming to some agreement on not only what nature is but how to preserve and sustain it. No other living creature is confronted with the dilemma and responsibility of this awareness.

Act like the spirit you are. See and feel the life of the forest. Enter its heart and partake of its unfolding in springtime.

Spring leafout: sycamore, cottonwod, and oaks.

An immature green heron

By engaging in a dialogue with nature, we become intimate with the wild, which in its otherness defines our uniqueness as humans and thereby our attendant responsibilities.

Nature is resilient, capable of recovering from disturbance and catastrophe. Yet this resilience has its limits, as we've learned from the extinction of the ivory-billed woodpecker and passenger pigeon, and the near-extinction of many other species. Our task is to know what those limits are, and to adjust our activities – all of which collide with nature to some degree – before irreversible damage occurs.

Resting for tomorrow's flight northward

April sunset over Missouri River bluffs

Adam Smith's landmark essay of 1776, The Wealth of Nations, extolled the virtues of pursuing one's economic self-interests; what is beneficial to the individual also accrues to the benefit of society he proclaimed. Since then, this belief has largely ruled our collective economic life and individual behavior. But if we do not simultaneously consider and act on what is good for the earth, we are on the road to our individual and collective ruin.

Legendary conservationist Aldo Leopold wrote in 1949: "A system of conservation based solely on economic self-interest is hopelessly lopsided. It tends to ignore, and thus eventually eliminate, many elements in the land community that lack commercial value, but that are (as far as we know) essential to its healthy functioning." More than 60 years later, his words fail to be understood or heeded by many who influence and control the use of our land – our earth, our home.

Double-crested cormorants and painted turtle

Shooting star (*Dodecatheon meadia*)

The first flowers of spring seem to say, "enough of drab, dead winter!   Let me show you the joy and beauty of life's renewal."

A love of nature acquired early may remain for a lifetime. But such good fortune doesn't fall to everyone. Writer Richard Louv coined the term "nature-deficit disorder" to characterize those with little awareness, knowledge, or love of nature. This state of consciousness, Louv believes, is all too common today among both children and adults. The resulting "deficit" reduces our ability, individually and societally, to effectively understand and deal with environmental issues – and thereby our own well being and survival as a species.

Discovering a wonder that will persist for a lifetime.

The doe signals with her eyes, ears and nose that she is aware of my presence. But she is cautious of leaving her fawn, which is hidden in the lush bottomland vegetation behind her. This is her home, her nursery. I am an intruder. Although I intend no harm, she doesn't know that. She responds according to her inherent instruction set: to safeguard the fawn, leaving it only as a last resort.

The doe and her fawn entered our suburban yard closely pursued by a large dog. As the fawn settled silently into a soft bed of violets and iris, the doe glanced nervously behind her. She then ran off, trying her best to lead the pursuer away. We took it upon ourselves to watch over the fawn, carefully from a distance, until the doe returned in the evening to reclaim her own.

Garden fawn

Great blue heron

The long-legged wading birds hold a special fascination for me. Perhaps it is because they, like me, are fishermen. Or perhaps it is because of other things within me I don't fully understand. "We love the things we love for what they are," wrote Robert Frost.

28

Each step taken along the sunken log is slowly, quietly deliberate for this great blue heron – a ghost in slow motion. But in a blink, his spear-like bill can dart into the water to return a squigling fish.

Great blue heron

Pelicans perform a "ballet" in unison to cooperatively drive fish.

If you reduce nature to nothing but anecdotal curiosity, you will miss its essence. Albert Einstein wrote: "There are two ways to live your life. One is as though nothing is a miracle. The other is as though everything is a miracle." If you've ever watched a sunset, you will know which path to follow.

Nature is not something that lies 'out there' beyond the pale. It is woven into the fabric of our being.

Ring-billed gulls over pelicans

Ring-billed gulls

Notice everything. The everyday is extraordinary.

Has society become a captive of the electronic age? Among many, digital devices have become an obsession. All of these wonders are truly magnificent and irresistable, and have almost magically become extensions of the human mind. But have we subordinated our consciousness to them, and in so doing relinquished our sense of connection to nature – from which our whole being and spirit is born?

Common snipe

Red-winged blackbird

Science has confirmed that the earth was not created in six days – contrary to the literal interpretation of the Holy Scriptures. Nevertheless, something or some One had to set the creational process, evolution, in motion.

The eyes of creatures are portals through which we can glimpse eternity.

Tufted titmouse

Pond sunset

Why this earth of whirling sky and water? Why anything at all? I know not the answers. But while I'm beholding its wonders, I'll pretend – no, *acknowledge* – it was created just for me and all who can appreciate it.

"*There is a time in every man's education* when he arrives at the conviction that envy is ignorance; that imitation is suicide; that he must take himself for better for worse as his portion; that though the wide universe is full of good, no kernel of nourishing corn can come to him but through his toil bestowed on that plot of ground which is given to him to till. The power which resides in him is new in nature, and none but he knows what that is which he can do, nor does he know until he has tried."—*Ralph Waldo Emerson*

American avocet

Bur oak in winter mist

In your journey, behold the earth's beauty and find joy in it.

Short-eared owls spend a few months here in the winter where they frequent large open fields. I view their presence in my 'neighborhood' as a priviledge akin to a miracle, for otherwise I would have to undertake the improbable journey to the Canadian tundra to see them.

Short-eared owl

We are the only species that, if it chooses, can save what it might otherwise destroy. Our collective responsibility, to both nature and ourselves, is thus to make informed choices that spring from an informed understanding and love of nature.

Each parcel of land listed in the platte book is owned by someone. But the landscape belongs to poets, dreamers and anyone who can appreciate it; let the real ownership lie where it will.

Pelicans beneath the bluffs

Cattle egret

Why all this diversity in nature? Is not the occurrence of three species of white wading birds in my neighborhood not duplication of evolutionary effort? Of course, in asking this question, we are noting only the whiteness of their feathers – and perhaps a few other visual similarities. But it requires much more to understand the uniqueness of each species' true place, or functional role, in the biosphere – and thus their importance to the integrity of the earth and thereby our own well being.

Snowy egret

Tanglewood

A geometric tangle of dead redcedar branches forms a life-giving substrate for mosses, lichens, and decomposing fungi. Nature is about endless cycles of birth and death.

The Missouri River bottoms were once mantled with magnificent forests of cottonwood, silver maple, sycamore, and other flood-tolerant hardwoods. These forests now cover only a small fraction of their former area. Today the river's floodplain is largely comprised of corn and soybean fields. The course of the river itself has been narrowed and its velocity and depth increased by diversion structures and dredging. Although this has greatly benefited river commerce and floodplain agriculture, it has reduced wetland wildlife habitat to a slim shadow of its original extent.

Bottomland hardwood forest in the Missouri River floodplain

Peace and tranquility can be found, I believe, through a genuine meeting with some of the creatures we share the earth with. You will know them by their quietude and thoughtful demeanor. Martin Buber instructs that "...being at rest in one's own self, to breach the barriers of the self and to come out from ourselves" requires us to "meet with essential otherness."

Pelicans consorting with double-crested cormorants

Tin-sided barn on the
Missouri River floodplain,
Moniteau County.

"Earring woman," Farmer's Market, Columbia

The marketplace and agriculture are emblamatic of our cultural evolution from a simple nomadic subsistance to the complexities of modern-day life. The new life has brought us much materially and freed us from the drudgery and insecurity of a primitive lifestyle. Few if any would want to turn the clock back. Nevertheless, some of us sense that something is missing – emanating from an immutable voice lying deep within us. The feeling dimly recalls the "ghost dances" the Lakota so tragically performed in 1890 at Wounded Knee. These dances were a spiritual call, a lamenting plea for the return and restoration of their people to their former way of life. Even today a saying darkly persists among Native Americans that "an Indian can reside in the city, but he can never live there." Perhaps those who have not had a *lived experience* with nature, especially during childhood, are slightly impoverished. And maybe that impoverishment is the emptiness that some feel in their lives today.

49

On their northward migration, the snow geese arrive here in late winter, sometimes in enormous flocks. But it's only a brief stopover on their way to the Arctic tundra. There are two color phases of this bird: white and dark (facing page right, formerly called the blue goose).

Above: This dark phase snow goose, apparently injured during migration and left behind by her flock, remained in our area until late spring.

Willows in winter

"The reason why the world lacks unity and lies broken and in heaps is because man is disunited with himself." *–Ralph Waldo Emerson*

Man's language, culture and tools set him apart from all other creatures. But that he alone knows this, perhaps best defines the difference.

Pintail ducks

Redbud (*Cercis canadensis*) in an oak grove.

We are born into nature and connected to all the living elements of Mother Earth through our evolutionary history.

Despite their beautiful plumage and striking crest, the coarse vocalizations of the blue jay betray its close relationship to the crow. Like the gray squirrel (p. 93), acorns are important in the blue jay's diet. But they are more effective at dispersing acorns than squirrels because, over a season, jays can carry them in larger numbers over longer distances (a mile or more) from their source. In doing so, they disperse acorns to relatively open habitats, which are more favorable for the growth and survival of the shade-intolerant oak seedling than under a forest canopy. The jay's expandable cheeks, which can accomodate up to 20 acorns (depending on acorn size) allow it to efficiently disperse acorns. Similar to squirrels, the jay caches its acorns beneath the leaf litter.

Blue jay

Above: Wood duck pair on nesting box; right: female with brood .

Spring is the season of rebirth
and renewal. If we're fortunate, we'll behold its
unfolding about 70 times – more or less. I treasure
each as though it were my last.

Lie down where the wood duck rests. Let the stillness of the water and the peace of wild things comfort you.

Wood duck pond

Black maple (*Acer nigrum*)

Ignorance of the earth is not conducive to its conservation and preservation. Knowledge of the earth and the collective will to intelligently apply it is urgently needed to save it, our home, from our own destructive excesses.

Treasure the moment. It is unique and will never appear again in exactly the same way.

Missouri River floodwater one second after sunset

Above: Oppossum; left: American kestrel (sparrow hawk).

Look gently into the eyes of any creature and you will see yourself, and eternity, reflected from within. "The consciousness of each of us is evolution looking at itself and reflecting upon itself," wrote Teilhard de Chardin.

These quiet giants, with 9-foot wing spans, create a nearly inaudible "silky-hiss" in flight. When they pass low overhead and near, you can hear their voices as they speak to each other in low gentle tones. Like old friends, I await their return each spring and autumn to engage in the conversation.

Quiet moment

Yearlings in pond at evening

When they come to the pond in the evening it is transformed by their presence. As we watch, they become a silent conversation, a communion; their presence speaks for us.

By September the fawn's spots have faded, soon to completely disappear. As the seasons change, so too everything within them. In nature, as in our own lives, change is the only constant.

Late summer fawn

Barn in the Missouri River breaks, a relic from another era.

In 1900, about 39 percent of the U.S. population lived on family farms. Now only about 2 percent do – and among those only half depend on farming for their primary income. Most of us today reside in urban enclaves far removed from the source of our physical sustenance. As a society, we've thus largely lost any direct connection to the land and any intimate sense of our dependency on it.

Back in 1908, it didn't take much to persuade country folks that a better life was awaiting them in Henry Ford's factory building Model T's. They left the farm in droves for the city, and most never looked back. A direct connection between the people and the land was thereupon largely lost — along with attendant understandings.

Bygone era

Forest canopy in spring

Forget the notion that all of these new technological marvels of recent have much to do with assuring our future. First we need to care for the earth in a way that assures *it* has a future.

As I watched the yellow-billed cuckoo, I was struck by both his beauty and spirit – a feathered spirit. In that moment I was reminded of Teilhard de Chardin's words that we are spiritual beings on a human journey.

Yellow-billed cuckoo

Monarch butterfly nectaring on bull thistle (*Cirsium vulgare*)

The monarch butterfly seems a miracle of nature. After migrating several thousand miles northward from the mountains of Mexico to southern Canada, these delicate insects return within the same year to again over-winter in Mexico. Although the northward journey involves several generations of monarchs, the return migration is completed by a single generation.

Caterpillar of the monarch butterfly (left) feeding on common milkweed (*Asclepias syriaca*; milkweed flower (right). Ingesting the toxic milkweed leaf renders the caterpillar unpalatable to its predators.

Red-bellied woodpecker

The birds around us are seen by some as meer curiosities, by others as something to be noted in a mental or written list – as if they were obligatory acquisitions; for others they may go largely unnoticed. Alternatively, all living things can be perceived more completely by meeting them in genuine dialogue. Although as real as any audible response, nature's reply explains philosopher Martin Buber, lies below the threshold of language.

Dickcissel

Orchard oriole

Painted turtles

In springtime, turtles awaken from the torpor of hibernation and seek the warmth of the sun while queued on a floating log.

The great diversity of living things keeps the earth biologically healthy and thereby us too.

Bullfrog

Above: Red-tailed hawk in pursuit;
below: tail feathers.

Yesterday I found a dead red-tailed hawk lying beneath a cottonwood and pondered the cause of his demise. Given that his fresh corpse lay within the wildlife refuge, I thought it unlikely he had been shot. Then I realized that his repose was within 50 yards of a bald eagle nest with an eagle sitting thereupon and a mate perched nearby. Two days earlier I observed a red-tail hovering near the nest. Perhaps the dead hawk at my feet was the intruder and the eagles, growing intolerant of his threat, dispatched him. Nature is dispassionate. Not even predators, the 'top dogs' of the wild, are immune from the threat of others of their ilk.

Red-tailed hawks: (right) on a freshly killed hen mallard; (below) keeping a watchfull eye.

Lifting off

Caring for the earth is a corollary of the golden rule.

The everyday becomes extraordinary when we are fully present to it, beholding it mindfully, and in open dialogue with its mysteries and wonder.

Pelican reflections, late afternoon

Team of Belgians

"All landscapes are constructed" argues Anne Whiston Spurn. "Garden, forest, city and wilderness are shaped by rivers and rain, plants and animals, human hands and minds. They are phenomena of nature *and* products of culture."

"Perhaps you have noticed that even in the very lightest breeze you can hear the voice of the cottonwood tree; this we understand is its prayer to the Great Spirit, for not only men, but all things and all beings pray to Him continually in differing ways." *—Black Elk*

Above: Eastern cottonwood (*Populus deltoides*) leaves; right: cottonwood sentinels, Missouri River floodplain.

Flowering dogwood (*Cornus florida*) beneath white oaks (*Quercus alba*). Although the dogwood will never grow large enough to yield a 2x4, it is nevertheless a part of the ecological integrity of this forest.

The earth is the "great integrity" said Lao Tzu. He warned that to allow the violation of this integrity by those who have the most power and wealth is certain to bring disaster. Although his warning came 2,600 years ago, the message today remains the same – albeit now ever more urgent. Whether based on said Lao Tzu.ancient philosophy or modern scientific findings, our individual and collective consciences should be telling us we are long overdue to heed the message.

I love this earth dearly, want to see and feel its beauty each day, am distressed at seeing or hearing about its further loss of integrity – even when such losses occur in distant places. My love and concern spring from values born in my neighborhood, my "home range" as the wildlife biologists call it. That is why it is so deeply personal; there is nothing distant or abstract about it.

Thin-leaved coneflower (*Rudbeckia triloba*)

Bottomland barn illuminated in winter light

This old barn stands as a monument to its own history. But now gone is the glow of light from within at milking time in winter. Late afternoon sun continues to illuminate its story, one that repeated every day for perhaps most of a century.

Each sunset is a gift, a celestial reassurance of tomorrow.

Golden sunset over Missouri River wetlands

A pectoral sandpiper stops off on his way to the Canadian Arctic.

Every living thing arrives at birth with an instruction set for fulfilling its primal purpose.

Societal objectives behind creating parks, wildlife refuges and natural areas are ostensibly to preserve and protect native species and biodiversity, while also providing outdoor recreational opportunities for people. But beneath it all, I believe their deepest underlying value lies in their contribution to preserving the human body, mind and spirit.

Green-winged teal

American plum (*Prunus americana*)

There is no such thing as seeking God, Martin Buber tells us, for there is nothing in which He cannot be found.

Care for the earth and it will care for us. Let us not squander its bounty and thus our future.

Morning mist

White oak catkins (the male, pollen-bearing flowers) at full maturity during leafout.

Learn about the trees, stars, quilting, molecular motion, planting a garden, or whatever interests you. Nothing is unimportant. Follow your passion and share your joy and knowledge of it with others. This is not only your fulfillment but ours as well.

Perhaps our love of music is born of some primal connection to the melodies and choruses of songbirds, frogs, crickets and the sound of wind in the trees – all long ago imprinted on our genetic code. Music and nature said Schopenhauer are "...two different expressions of the same thing" – both lying within our innermost consciousness.

A yellow-breasted chat sings from his willow perch.

Wetland elegy

I look for the beauty around me every day. I am mindful and fully present to it through the silent dialogue I have with it – which is the source of its lasting influence.

The earth is my home and will remain so until I fly away to the other.

Blue-winged teal

While I love the bottomlands along the meandering Big Muddy, the adjacent uplands offer a different perspective. Interspersed among broad bands of oak forest are finger ridges of fescue pasture. This mosaic is the domain of the gray squirrel and wild turkey, which share their habitat with other animals including deer, raccoon, fox, coyote, cottontail, oppossum, and a myriad of songbirds.

Gray squirrels and oaks are mutually dependent. In autumn, the squirrels store acorns in scattered caches beneath the leaf litter. Because they often don't eat all they store, some acorns germinate to develop into seedlings. Burial beneath the leaf litter protects acorns from winter desiccation and freezing, and from predation by insects and other animals. Without squirrels, some believe, there would be few oaks and oak forests.

Above left: A northern red oak seedling three weeks after germination (7/8 actual size). Its leaves are just beginning to unfold. Because root growth begins before shoot growth, root development is ahead of shoot growth at this stage; above right: a gray squirrel.

Twelve-spot skimmer dragonfly

*In the heat of the late summer doldrum*s, nature often seems to have grown tired of fully showing herself. It is then that I most appreciate the dragonflies. Not only are they colorful, but also astonishly aerobatic. Flying forward, backward and sideways, they seem to defy the laws of physics as they change direction in a blink – no doubt an adaptation to catching other insects in flight.

94

The dragonflies called darners are so-named because their body is shaped like a darning needle, i.e. wider at the head and thorax than along their ten-segment abdomen. The one below is the colorful blue form of the common green darner – as if its flight magic were not enough to charm us.

Green darner dragonfly

Turkey Vulture

A part of a creature's beauty lies in its role in the scheme of things. Lying more than skin deep, that part is often invisible and misunderstood.

Evening light turns the dead cottonwood a warm yellow, in any other time a dull, weathered gray. Its radiance beckons turkey vultures to their evening roost.

Turkey vulture's evening roost

Scissor-tailed flycatcher, an occasional visitor from the Great Plains.

His unusually long tail was recognizable a quarter-mile down the road from where he was perched. Although the scissor-tailed flycatcher seldom frequents my area, individuals occassionally show up as 'wanderers' – as the ornithologists call them. Normally at home in the Oklahoma and Texas reaches of the Great Plains, this one stayed around a large soybean field along the Missouri River bottoms for about 10 days. The presence of this beautiful, exotic creature momentarily tempted me to reduce him to anecdotal curiosity. But when I approached him on foot to get a closer look, we acknowledged each other briefly when he glanced down at me from his perch. At that moment, a barely discernable twitch of his folded wings betrayed his nervousness. Seconds later he flew off – but not before we glimpsed each other, neither of us completely knowable to the other.

"All actual life is encounter" proclaims philosopher Martin Buber. The encounters are the events of our personal everyday life. No event is greater or smaller than another; we are addressed by each of them equally. Our task, he instructs, is to hallow our relationship with the everyday.

Spotted sandpiper

Pelican congregation

Losses in the "great integrity" may not always make the six o'clock news. But that doesn't mean none have occurred. Indifference to the state of our environment is a luxury we can ill afford.

Stretching the earth's resources including clean air and water beyond their elastic limits seems to some to be acceptable, even expected. Should we not recoil from this *modus operandi* before we start gasping for our last breath!

Sextet

Field of henbit (*Lamium amplexicaule*) on the Missouri River floodplain at McBaine

" *I know nothing of a world and of worldly life* that separate us from God. What is designated that way is life with an alienated *It*-world..." *–Martin Buber.*

An afternoon at Lucy's, the social and cultural center of McBaine. This hamlet lies along Perche Creek on the Missouri River floodplain near Eagle Bluffs Conservation Area. Here local folks mix with bikers and hikers from nearby KATY Trail to enjoy good food, libation and sometimes live entertainment.

What'd you say your name was masked man?

Let me get a closer look at those teeth.

No need to get your hackles up!

Nice meeting you; I'm leaving now.

Bessie's first (and last) raccoon caper; neither animal was harmed in the encounter.

Our animals are a part of us and woven into the human-nature relationship. Although dogs evolved from the gray wolf, they split off from them about 135,000 years ago. Dogs are believed to have further evolved through a close, mutually beneficial relationship with early man that began more than 50,000 years ago. Some scientists believe the relationship involved the *coevolution* of man and dog – meaning that each influenced the evolution and nature of the other. From the outset, this partnership was inherently compatible. Both possessed highly evolved intelligence and cooperative, altruistic behavior – a combination of traits rare in the animal world. Not surprisingly then, no other animal comes close to the dog as friend and helper to man.

Whether interacting with us as herders, hunters, protectors, or guiding the unsighted, they do it with a wagging tail attached to a heart born to please. Although we're not exactly sure where our late Bess (3/4 boxer and 1/4 English bulldog) fit into a service to mankind, we suspect she functioned primarily as family parapsychologist. Within our family, she was an important link to nature – a member of the 'other' that we could understand only incompletely – yet she was an authentic part of us.

Bess, in remembrance

Pin oak

Hickory

Chinkapin oak

White oak

Bibliography

Buber, Martin. (1970) *I and Thou*. Walter Kaufmann, trans. (from Ich and Du, 1923). Reprint 1996, Simon and Schuster, New York. 185 pp.

Dale, Ralph Alan. (2005) *Tao Te Ching: A New Translation and Commentary*. Barnes and Noble, New York. 284 pp.

Emerson, Ralph Waldo. (1836) Nature. In: *The Best of Ralph Waldo Emerson: Essays, Poems, Addresses*, pp. 73-116. Walter J. Black, New York. 281 pp.

Friedman, Maurice. (2002) *Martin Buber: the Life of Dialogue*, 4th edition. Routledge, New York. 404 pp.

Frost, Robert. (1971) *The Road Not Taken, A Selection of Robert Frost's Poems*. Henry Holt. New York. 282 pp.

Huxley, Thomas H. (1869) NATURE: Aphorisms by Goethe. Nature 1(1).

Johnson, Paul S., Stephen R. Shifley, and Robert Rogers. (2009) *The Ecology and Silviculture of Oaks*, 2nd edition. CAB International, Oxfordshire, UK. 580 pp.

Kramer, Kenneth Paul and Mechthild Gawlick. (2003) *Martin Buber's I and Thou, Practicing Living Dialogue*. Paulist Press, New York. 215 pp.

Leopold, Aldo. (1949) *A Sand County Almanac and Sketches Here and There*. Oxford University Press, New York. 228 pp.

Louv, Richard. (2011) *The Nature Principle: Human Restoration and the End of Nature-Deficit Disorder*. Algonquin Books, Chapel Hill, North Carolina. 317 pp.

McLean, Scott. (1996) "The water runs over the words." In: *The Idea of the Forest, German and American Perspectives on the Culture and Politics of Trees*, pp. 163-187. K. L. Schultz and K. S. Calhoon, eds. Peter Lang Publishing, New York. 221 pp.

Muir, John. (1938) *John of the Mountains: The Unpublished Journals of John Muir*, L. M. Wolfe, ed. Reprint. University of Wisconsin Press, Madison, 1966. 459 pp.

Neihardt, John G. (1961) *Black Elk Speaks*. University of Nebraska Press, Lincoln. 298 pp.

Schleidt, Wolfang M. and Shalter, Michael D. (2003) Co-evolution of humans and canids, an alternative view of dog domestication: Homo Homini Lupus? *Evolution and Cognition* 9(1):57-72.

Schopenhauer, Arthur. (1819) *The World as Will and Representation*. Vol. I. E. F. J. Payne, trans. Reprint 1969, Dover Publications, New York. 534 pp.

Smith, Adam. (1776) *An Inquiry into the Nature and Causes of the Wealth of Nations, Volume 1*. W. Strahan and T. Cadell, London.

Spurn, Anne Whiston. (1996) Constructing nature: the legacy of Frederick Law Olmsted. In: *Uncommon Ground, Rethinking the Human Place in Nature*, pp. 97-113. William Cronon, ed. W. W. Norton, New York. 561 pp.

Teilhard de Chardin, Pierre. (1959) *The Phenomenon of Man*. Harper and Row, New York. 319 pp.

_____ (1964) *The Future of Man*. Harper and Row, New York. 332 pp.

_____ (1971) *Christianity and Evolution*. Harcourt Brace Jovanich, New York. 255 pp.

Thoreau, Henry David. (1854) *Walden*. Reprint. Shambhala Publications, Boston, 2004. 303 pp.

Wilson, Edward O. (2012) *The Social Conquest of Earth*. Liveright Publishing, New York. 330 pp.

37543903R00064

Made in the USA
Lexington, KY
06 December 2014